COACHING UNDER 10s

A COMPLETE COACHING COURSE

by Tino Stoop, KNVB Academy

REEDSWAIN PUBLISHING

Author
Tino Stoop

Co-workers Andries Jonker, Johan van Geijn, Nico
Romeijn, Raymond Verheijen and Henk van de
Wetering
With thanks to Erwin Koeman, Willem-II Tilburg and
soccer club Sarto Tilburg

Illustrations
Tino Stoop

Photographs
Jan de Koning

Editing
Paul Driesen

Translation
Dave Brandt - Experteam

**Library of Congress
Cataloging - in - Publication Data**

Coaching Under 10s
A Complete Coaching Course
Stoop, Tino

ISBN No. 1-59164-066-0
Lib. of Congress Catalog No. 2003095177
© 2003

Printed by
DATA REPRODUCTIONS
Auburn, Michigan

Reedswain Publishing
612 Pughtown Road
Spring City, PA 19475
800.331.5191
www.reedswain.com
info@reedswain.com

CONTENTS

FOREWORD

It was a pleasure for me to help with the making of the CD for young soccer players in the under-10 age group. During the shooting I became convinced that the coaching methods, as shown on the CD and described in this book, are an excellent way of helping U10s to learn how to play soccer better.

Many U10 players have been members of their soccer club for at least 2 years and have attended lots of coaching sessions and played dozens of matches. Nevertheless, it is very important that they continue to develop their technical skills. This means practicing shooting, scoring and defending, and keeping and winning possession as individuals and as a team, in ways that are appropriate to their age group, with the aim of mastering the art of ball control and gaining their first insights into the game of soccer.

At this age, young players lay the foundation for their soccer careers. How their careers develop will differ from player to player. Some will play simply for pleasure, while others may eventually represent their country. In this phase, however, every youngster must be given the opportunity to learn to play soccer. All of them must participate to the best of their ability. The U10s practice the technical skills they need to learn, and play the first simple games involving keeping and winning possession as a team. As in the highest levels of soccer, each coaching session ends with a small sided game. Just as it should.

Naturally, equipment is needed, but youngsters enjoy their coaching sessions and learn how to play soccer properly, so money used to buy equipment is money well spent.

Some time is needed to set everything up before a coaching session can start, but as a result the session runs more smoothly.

At first sight, supervising youngsters using the circuit model appears difficult. From personal experience, however, I can assure coaches that this is not so. The youngsters quickly become familiar with the circuit model and soon recognize the individual elements.

I hope you enjoy coaching U10 players as much as I did, and I wish you lots of enjoyment.

Erwin Koeman   Eindhoven, May 2002

Boys and girls who like to play soccer usually join a club. At the club they are under the supervision of a coach. A coach who wants to do his job properly must address a number of questions such as "What are the characteristics of this age group?," "What is the best way to structure a coaching session?," "What is the best system to use?," and "What can young players learn?" This book has been written to provide answers to these questions.

A key aspect of the learning plan is that it must mesh with the play culture of the youngsters. Youngsters often play on the street and in the school yard without any adult supervision, sometimes for hours on end. They often play small sided games.

At coaching sessions, the players are divided into 3 groups. 3 fields are set up, on which 4 to 6 players can carry out soccer drills. These soccer drills have simple rules and young players can carry them out on their own.

The youngsters rotate from field to field, carrying out a different drill on each one. Finally they play a small sided game of 4v4 on 2 fields. This system is known as the circuit model.

Coaching with the circuit model

The aim of the soccer drills in this book is to give youngsters a grasp of as many different facets of the game of soccer as possible. The coaching aspects are based on the principles of street soccer: small groups, rules suited to the level of the players, lots of ball contacts and thus learning by repetition. To achieve this, youngsters must be able to play simultaneously on a number of adjacent fields. But how can this be achieved? If your team is distributed over 3 fields, there might be 5 players per drill!

There are a number of obvious practical problems:

* How do I start, how do I change to another drill and how do I end the session?
* What must the youngsters be able to do in order to play without supervision?
* How can I supervise 3 soccer drills at the same time?

The circuit model offers solutions to these problems. At the same time it must be remembered that it is a means of enabling youngsters to gain the most benefit, and is not an objective in itself! An important precondition for the success of the circuit model is that the youngsters must be able to carry out a soccer drill without supervision. Can they do the following themselves:

* Start a soccer drill?
* Apply the rules of the game and rules of behavior (e.g. wait until everyone is ready again after a goal has been scored) or modify them?
* Swap functions (first defender, then attacker)?

"Surely U10s can't do all that?" is a comment that is often heard. Experience, however, has shown that they can. People often forget that at this age youngsters have a number of years of school behind them. Schools increasingly encourage their pupils to develop self-reliance. They often work in groups. In general, soccer clubs have failed to profit from this. Youngsters in this age group are capable of a lot more than is often assumed.

Nevertheless, it does take some time before the youngsters become familiar with the circuit model. In most cases, the first fruits of this form of organization can be seen after just 2 training sessions. Chapter 4 of this book deals with the circuit model in detail.

Learning young...

On his daily walk, Frits, a retired teacher, passes a field where youngsters often play soccer. Today is no exception. 5 youngsters are taking penalties. Frits stands and watches for a while. He soon sees which players try to place the ball and which ones simply kick it as hard as they can. Frits asks them if he can take a penalty too. They agree. Frits then shoots calmly into the right corner of the goal, just inside the post. Frits resumes his walk. When he passes the field again on his way back, the youngsters are busy practicing placing their penalty kicks in the right corner of the goal.

U10 players are between 8 and 10 years old. At many clubs, boys and girls are coached together. The level of soccer skills varies widely, regardless of gender.

The players

Clearly, these youngsters are not all the same. Nevertheless, a number of typical characteristics can be distinguished, and it is important to know what they are. This is especially true when a coach has relatively little experience with players in this age group.

An overview of these characteristics is therefore given here, together with relevant tips for coaches.

- The youngsters love to play. They do things for the pleasure of doing them. They should therefore be given the opportunity to practice all kinds of skills and solutions to soccer problems in a play environment. Such an approach is soon reflected in an improved ability to control the ball.

- They have an urge to imitate. Every new movement results partly from imitation. Demonstration is therefore very important. The coach should demonstrate clearly whenever possible.

- They have a lot of endurance. This means that they can spend a lot of time playing soccer. They must have as many ball contacts as possible. They learn by repetition. They also need to expend a lot of energy to gain maximum enjoyment. Well timed rest periods are therefore essential.

- They are capable of saying what they do and do not like. This can provide the coach with information about how they experience their soccer. It is important to ask them why they do or don't like something.

- They are direct. This means that scoring goals during soccer drills has a major influence on their attitude. It is important to explain how to score goals and points.

- They are more prepared to cooperate, with a view to scoring goals, than U10s. They gradually come to appreciate the advantages of a square pass to a player in a better position.

The coach and the parents

Not only youngsters but also adults are present (on the field and in the locker room). These adults have an important task. Fortunately, some parents follow the soccer progress of their child. The enthusiasm of parents is crucial to their children's enthusiasm for the game. However, many parents are not content simply to provide encouragement. They try to project their own emotions onto their children. Encouraging words become instructions and before long there are twice as many coaches on the side line as players on the field.

In addition, some parents regard the match result and the position in the league table as more important than their children's enjoyment of the game and the progress they are making. The involvement of such parents can take many forms. They may try to influence the way in which the rules of the game are applied and thus the match result.

Both coaches and parents are responsible for the enjoyment experienced by their own team and the opposing team! The coach has the important but very difficult task of ensuring that parents understand the role they have to play during the match, and the role of the coach relative to the players. The emphasis is on the learning process and the youngsters' enjoyment of the game. Children learn fastest in a secure environment, where they have the freedom to discover the game for themselves.

Young players are helped in this by one person: the coach. The structures must be very clear. If they are not, confusion arises and the youngsters no longer know where they are. Young players find it exciting to be encouraged. Parents are necessary and welcome spectators. Their help to the coach is often indispensable. As long as the youngsters need help to get ready for the match, parents are essential in the locker room! The learning structure must be viewed as the next step to independence and self-motivation. Give the young player a chance!

Only one person helps young players to discover the game: the coach.

3 BASICS OF SOCCER AT THE U10 LEVEL

The pleasure of doing things

Children love to play. They do things for the pleasure of doing them. They should therefore be given the opportunity to practice all kinds of skills and solutions to soccer problems in a playful environment. Such an approach is soon reflected in an improved ability to handle the ball. The recognition of this first age-group-related characteristic is very important, because it serves as the starting point for choosing suitable soccer drills.

What does 'playfully occupied' mean? Everyone has a different answer. Teachers think of infants playing with blocks. Coaches of young soccer players think of games of 7v7 on a Saturday morning. Parents think of the play house in the yard.

The character of the game

'Playfully occupied' describes the character of an activity: its playfulness. Children can lose themselves in a game of soccer. Just think of the eternal problem of getting home on time to eat when the game is not yet decided. The element of play seems to be of great value in the learning process. Learning seems to happen of its own accord: 'playing is learning' and 'learning is playing.'

For young soccer players, the play aspect of the game must be maintained. This is always the case when each of the following 4 elements is present:
1. A recognizable objective.
2. The rules of the game.
3. The equipment needed to be able to play the game (for example, the ball and the goals).
4. A play-oriented approach.

The presence of just one of these factors is sometimes considered sufficient to justify calling an activity a game. This is too little. All of the 4 elements must be present before an activity can be termed a game. A play-oriented approach may be regarded as the prerequisite for realizing the other 3 elements. If the coach makes the right choices with regard to these 4 elements the game remains enjoyable for the players. The game is self perpetuating - and repetition is a way of learning!

A game area is a collection of simplified soccer drills and games incorporating a common soccer problem.

1. A recognizable objective

Every game has a recognizable objective. A golfer wants to hole the ball, and a volleyball player wants to place the ball in the opposition's court in such a way that it cannot be returned. In soccer, the objective is either to score a goal or to prevent the opposition from scoring one.

Regardless of the number of players in each team, the objective remains the same. There are more soccer drills than just small sided games. For example, youngsters can compete against each other at taking penalties, taking turns in shooting at one goal. Sometimes they just kick a ball around. Analysis of small sided games reveals 4 main game areas:

1. Shooting at a goal.
2. Scoring and preventing others from scoring.
3. Keeping possession and winning possession as an individual.
4. Keeping possession and winning possession as a team.

If there are only a few players, more scoring chances are created. This makes 4v4 an interesting and instructive game. The problem with U10s is that it is difficult for them to learn how to play soccer better in a small sided game of 7v7. In some cases even 4v4 causes problems. Often a scrum of players forms around the ball, which bobbles randomly hither and thither. This book describes 4 game areas to help youngsters to play soccer better.

An example of a simplified soccer drill is the shooting game. Scoring and defending are explained on the basis of the small sided game and are highlighted in a simplified soccer drill. The soccer problem in the game area scoring and defending is 'guiding the ball past the goalkeeper while the goalkeeper tries to prevent this.' Shooting - for instance shooting at cones - is closely related to scoring. The difference to 'real' scoring is the absence of a goalkeeper. Nevertheless, youngsters enjoy shooting at

Game Area	Theme line	Soccer problem
Shooting	Shooting drills	Shooting accurately
Scoring and Defending	Scoring drills	Scoring and defending
Keeping and winning possession as an individual	Keeping possession drills	Keeping possession while an opponent tries to win the ball
Keeping and winning possession as a team	Small sided drills	Combining to keep possession and score while opponents try to win the ball and prevent goals

cones and there is always a visible result! The shooting game is not a small sided game, but is a very suitable soccer drill for beginners. Shooting drills are simplified soccer drills with the emphasis on shooting. Scoring drills are soccer drills in which the emphasis is on scoring and defending. The game area keeping possession and winning possession as an individual can also be highlighted in simplified soccer drills. One example of a keeping possession drill is the 3-lives game: youngsters have to cross over a certain area with a ball at their feet while an opponent tries to kick the ball away or take possession of it. Simplified soccer drills with the emphasis on keeping possession and winning possession are keeping possession (individual) drills.

Finally the game area keeping possession and winning possession as a team is explained on the basis of the small sided game and highlighted in a simplified soccer situation in small sided drills.

The soccer drills that belong to a given game area can be organized in series so that the players can progress from easy to more difficult drills. Such a methodical series is referred to here as a theme line.

A theme line is a series of soccer drills and games derived from a certain game area.

Youngsters at this age have difficulty keeping a 'kick around' game going for any length of time. Without a coach to introduce variety, the game soon loses its excitement. The youngsters are helped to learn how to play together in small sided games, in which the team in possession has the most players (for example, 4v2). Several goals are placed on the end line. (If there is

only one goal, attacks tend to become bogged down in a mob of players.) These small sided games, with variations in the size of the field, the number of goals, the size of the scoring zone or the number of players, are incorporated in the circuit model.

Each simplified soccer drill therefore has a game objective. For the youngsters, this is visible in the results they achieve. It must be clear how goals can be scored and prevented. The players must be able to answer questions such as "How many points have you scored?" or "What is the score?" The results enable the coach to monitor the personal progress of the youngsters. The coach also has the option of making a drill harder or easier (see also chapter 6 - Soccer drills in practice).

The practical part of this book includes shooting, scoring, keeping possession and small sided drills. The diagram on page 7 gives a general overview of the game areas, theme lines and soccer problems.

Monitor the game objective

A variety of soccer problems are raised in the named game areas. As a result, the youngsters learn in play how to deal with soccer situations in a play environment. Initially, no technical instructions are given. The organization of the soccer drill is such that the soccer problem is immediately obvious to the players and they use the best available shooting technique to solve it. In the case of keeping possession in a small area, while a defender tries to win possession, the player with the ball positions himself between the ball and the defender. Instructions such as "Body between ball and defender" or "Make yourself as wide as possible" are unnecessary. This is to be expected at this stage of the players' development (see chapter 2 - Characteristics of U10s). They are unable to translate such instructions into soccer actions.

The described soccer drills give the youngsters the opportunity of experiencing what it means to be '2 footed.' The way in which the drills are presented stimulates them to acquire the ability to use both feet naturally in a play setting. In this phase the youngsters can choose, not the adults!

2. Rules of the game

The rules should always serve the purposes of the game and can be changed if required. Rules enable a drill to be carried out and must therefore be clear. In addition, there must be clear agreements on when to swap roles. For example: Change the goalkeeper after 5 unsuccessful shots. When the players learn a new drill, the coach must first monitor whether they carry it out in accordance with the rules. When the coach demonstrates a drill, he should explain the game objective in no more than 3 basic rules, so that the players can start the game as quickly as possible.

More specific rules can be introduced later.

When the players start carrying out a drill, one of the first tasks of the coach is to monitor whether the players understand the game objective. Are the rules clear?

3. The equipment needed to be able to play the game

A certain amount of equipment is necessary, such as a proper goal or a goal marked by 2 cones or a row of target cones. A ball, marker cones to define the field, etc. are also needed. These are all examples of equipment needed to carry out soccer drills. The equipment must be suited to the level of the players' skills. Distances and the size of the field play the most important role. How big is the field? How wide are the goals? The size and weight of the ball are also important. The organization of a soccer drill - and thus the choice of equipment - must be carefully considered and put into practice.

Set off from the starting gate

The proper equipment can enormously increase the enjoyment value of a drill. A proper goal with a net appeals more to the imagination than a goal marked by cones. The introduction of counter cones can also motivate defenders to win the ball as quickly as possible from dribblers.

A coach can make a drill harder or simpler by introducing organizational changes. A variety of options are available:
1) The field can be made bigger. It is then easier for the player with the ball to run into space (an abstract term for youngsters in this age group).
2) Goals marked by cones can be made smaller, so that it is harder to score from a distance. Or the goals can be made wider if the players are finding it difficult to score.
3) In the shooting game, the distance between the penalty spot and the goal can be shortened if the goalkeeper almost always saves the penalties.

All of these interventions influence the learning process of a soccer player without requiring much explanation from the coach. The players experience the changes directly. The changes therefore work quickly and effectively.

Clear and challenging organization ensures that the players can grasp and experience the game objective. Changing the organization is a good way of enabling soccer players to learn something new without any need for explanations.

4. A play-oriented approach

Objective, rules and equipment are of no use if the players are not receptive to the rules of the game. If they are unwilling to accept these rules, it is impossible to play properly.

When the rules are clearly understood, the players watch out for infringements themselves. They are their own referee. If a player of team A sends the ball out of play, a player of team B recovers the ball and sends it back into play. This also applies to other rules, such as not handling the ball. Youngsters also learn faster if they can shoot from the champion's cone (a special marker cone) at the cones of the player on the other side. The players learn to apply the rules themselves. In this way, space is created for a play-oriented approach. Youngsters seem to enjoy a lot of these soccer drills, which are often derived from small sided games.

A play-oriented approach

4 CIRCUIT MODEL

A coach must try to introduce his players to as many soccer drills as possible. In the circuit model, a number of fields are set up adjacent to each other so that more than one group can play at the same time. The following questions are frequently asked:

- What is a circuit model?
- Why use a circuit model?
- How long does it take to set everything up, make changes and take everything down?
- How can I introduce the circuit model during coaching sessions?
- What equipment do I need?

What is a circuit model?

The circuit model is a model for the organization of a practice session. The youngsters play in groups. The session starts with a game of tag or a kick around (as warm up) in a marked zone. Groups are then formed, each of which works through 3 different soccer drills (for example, a scoring, keeping possession and/or a small sided drill). The players complete one or 2 circuits. The session then closes with a small sided game. The same drills can be carried out during the next session.

The circuit model is a tool that helps youngsters to learn to play soccer better!

Why use a circuit model in coaching sessions?

For the players, it is better and more enjoyable to repeat a number of soccer drills briefly each week rather than just focusing on one drill for a longer time. Moreover, practice (repetition) makes perfect.

Advantages of the circuit model

1. The coaching is orientated to the world of the young players and provides lots of variation. All game areas can be included.
2. The players have lots of ball contacts (no problems with long waiting times).
3. The duration of the soccer drills is about 15 minutes, which is about equal to the attention span of the young players, i.e. the time that they can concentrate on one soccer problem.
4. Young players can work better together in small groups rather than one large one. The coach can focus on one group if he sees that it needs help.
5. Repetition of the same drills provides ample opportunities for learning.

The traditional picture of a coach in front of the group as a whole seems to be an easier option than setting up and organizing 3 different soccer drills. Initially this is so. Subsequently, however, the circuit model is easier. The variation and the greater challenge motivate the players and encourage them to play more independently.

As a result it is easier for the coach to maintain an overview, but at the same time it is less necessary for him to do so. Experience has shown that the initial sessions may be a little chaotic, but within 1 or 2 sessions the players are familiar with the organization. This model, therefore, need not be a barrier for anyone and is an interesting challenge for everyone.

However, the soccer drills must remain exciting. At first, a drill can be chosen that all the players can pick up easily. This gives the coach more time to focus on becoming accustomed to the circuit model. Each soccer drill can be adjusted in the following sessions, or replaced by another drill (from the same theme line). If a soccer drill is exciting, the players can carry it out 4 or 5 times in sequence without losing interest. Players become familiar with the structure of the soccer drill, can start the drill themselves and can sometimes set it up themselves. As a result, the coach has more time to monitor whether everything is organized properly and to help players to learn. Are the goals wide enough? Should the field be wider? Is the striker not too close to the goalkeeper? Do the players keep the ball close enough to their feet when they dribble? Does the player in the back and forth game check the position of the opposition's ball before passing to his teammate on the other side? All of these things play a role in the following coaching session.

Time

Preparation
A good coaching session starts with the preparation. This book gives a number of guidelines and practical examples. These can be useful in the first coaching sessions of the U10s. This does not mean that everything has to be learned by heart. On the contrary, you can take a work drawing with you onto the pitch. (You can keep this drawing in a plastic folder to prevent it from getting wet.) Standard Letter format is best for such drawings; details such as cones are clearly visible. The work drawing can be kept in a folder for use by other coaches in subsequent years. In this way an archive can be created.

It is advisable for the coaches of the U10s to reach agreements before the start of the season, for example about creating a coaching folder. Every coach can use this. It can also be presented as documentation to the commission for young players or the young players' coordinator if required.

Setup
Ideally, the fields will be set up before the session starts. This means that no time is wasted during the session. In practice, however, another team might already be using the pitch. In that case there are a number of options:

* The coaches who use the pitch on a given afternoon or evening can agree to make things easier for each other. For example, coach A may organize his session so that it ends with a small sided game on the field closest to the locker rooms, so coach B can set up the equipment he needs on the unused area of the pitch.

* At the start of the season, the coaching sessions can be scheduled so that equipment can be used by players in the same age groups. For example, 3 U10 teams can use the equipment first, and 3 others afterwards. Naturally the coaches must also coordinate their coaching themes.

* After a while, the players can help with setting up the field. There is always one player who remembers exactly how this or that must be done. At the next session, he is willing and eager to help the coach. A compliment from the coach, in the presence of the whole group, can have an enormously stimulating effect.

* In the initial stages, a few parents might also help. They are usually there to help their children to get into their soccer kit. With the help of a few extra copies of the work drawing, everything is soon in place. Moreover, in this way they become involved in the bigger picture.

A lot of time is lost if the equipment has to be set up during the coaching session. It is more efficient to put things away. The example illustrates this:

Step 1: Set up 2 large fields (40 x 20 yards) for a small sided game at the end of the coaching session.

Step 2: Within these fields, mark out fields A, B and C and D.

Step 3: After each element of the session, some of the equipment can be cleared away.

Step 4: The small sided game - the final element of the session - then only requires the goals to be set up (cones or 'real' 4v4 goals).

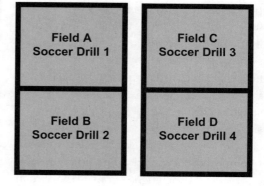

| Field A Soccer Drill 1 | Field C Soccer Drill 3 |
| Field B Soccer Drill 2 | Field D Soccer Drill 4 |

Changes

While a group is playing, the coach can change the field (for example, by making it wider or narrower). Changes can also be made when the groups move on from one element of the session to the next - at this age, youngsters are good at helping. After watching how it is done, they are able, for example, to take the cones used for the skittle game and position them for another soccer drill.

Cleaning up

It is extremely important that the players should learn that looking after the equipment and putting it away after the coaching session is a major aspect of their soccer development and education. The coach can present this as a game. 'The world record for cleaning up is...Let's see if we can improve on it today'. Within 2 minutes everything will be neatly arranged on the equipment cart. Monitor this from the very start!

Structure of the circuit model

Working with a circuit model requires a coach to invest a lot a time and energy, especially in the initial stages. Both the coach and the players have to learn to work with the model, and everyone must be given the necessary time to do this. Inexperienced coaches tend to worry that they will lose control of what is happening if the players are busy on 3 fields at the same time. It is comforting to know that the youngsters often adapt more quickly than the adults who are in charge of the session. During the second coaching session, most of the players are already familiar with the structure and organization. Just one word often suffices. The time lost during the first coaching sessions is more than won back in the course of the season.

Even for an experienced coach, it is a major task to start a session simultaneously on several fields. The numbers are not written in stone. If you have a group of, for example, ten players, then it is best to play on 2 fields. In other words, the division is done on the basis of the number of players needed for a given soccer drill, and not the number of fields that have been set up or the size of the group!

Three coaching sessions will now be described. They show how the sessions can be structured to allow the complete circuit model to be used. In other words, the focus is solely on the organizational format.

- The group consists of twelve youngsters
- They are unfamiliar with the circuit model
- The fields/equipment are set up before hand
- The session lasts 60 minutes
- Descriptions of the soccer drills are provided in chapter 6 (Soccer drills in practice).

Session 1

Time (min.)	Drill	Game area	Groups	Players/Grp
-10 - 0	Setting up the equipment			
0 - 5	Tag/kick around		1	12
5 - 20	Shooting game	Shooting	2	6
20 - 40	Customs game	Keeping possession and winning possession as an individual	2	6
40 - 55	Small sided game 4v4/2v2	All game areas	2	8+4
55 - 60	Cleaning up			

Activity 1: **Tag/kick around**

Organization: All of the youngsters can play a game of tag in an area measuring 15 x 15 yards. The youngsters can also kick the ball around in a larger area.

Reasons: A game of tag keeps the youngsters together in a group and prevents their enthusiasm from taking them in all directions. This can happen in a kick around, when there is a

Warming up with a game of tag

risk that they may use the equipment that has been set up. A joint start can give structure to the session at this age. Moreover the setup remains intact.

Activity 2: **Shooting game**

Organization: Take the youngsters to the field for the shooting game.

Reasons: Explain and demonstrate the game to all the players at the same time. They can then carry it out simultaneously in 2 groups.

Activity 3: **Customs game**

Organization: Call the players together and run to the 2 fields for the customs game. Demonstrate the game with 5 youngsters, then allow another player to take your place. Monitor whether the game runs smoothly. The 6 players who stood on the sideline then run to the second field and start to play the game there. Once again, monitor the progress of the game.

Reason: This is a new soccer drill. The demonstration is given for the whole group. Any questions can be cleared up.

Activity 4: Small sided game 4v4

Organization: Call the players together and ask them to collect the cones. The fields for the small sided game are set up at the start of the coaching session. If the fields are ready, distribute the practice vests. Allow the youngsters to play at once. After about twelve minutes the game can be stopped and the teams can move on.

Activity 5: Cleaning up and closing up together

Reasons: During the first session, explanations are given to the whole group and therefore only need to be given once. This 'central' approach means that teething problems can be solved with the whole group. After all, these are unfamiliar drills with new rules. The (novice) coach therefore does not need to

provide help at a number of different locations to keep the various soccer drills going. The organization is clear for both the coach and the players. Because this is the first coaching session, more time is needed to help the players to get started. Changeover, setting up and clearing away will also take more time. Usually the session is planned with one soccer drill from each theme line. For the following session a new drill is chosen from the small sided games theme line.

Explaining

Session 2

Time (min.)	Drill	Game area	Groups	Players/Grp
-10 - 0	Setting up the equipment			
0 - 5	Tag/kick around		1	12
5 - 25	Shooting game	Scoring and Defending	1	6
5 - 25	Customs game	Keeping and winning possession as an individual	1	6
25 - 40	Small sided drill (3v3)	Keeping possession and winning possession as a team	2	6
40 - 55	Small sided game (4v4/2v2)	All game areas	2	8+4
55 - 60	Cleaning up			

Activity 1:   Tag/kick around

Reasons:

Same tag game as in session 1. This element is familiar. The players can therefore start quickly. Explanations are unnecessary.

Activity 2:   Shooting game and Customs game

Organization:

These drills are also familiar from session 1. All players watch while a number of players demonstrate. Then distribute the whole group over the fields with the shooting game and customs game. The shooting game players can start. Accompany the group for the customs game and start them off. Change of drill after ten minutes.

Reasons:

A brief demonstration is sufficient. When the time to change drills arrives,

take the shooting game players to watch the customs game and let them watch while the game proceeds. When everyone knows how it is played, let the youngsters who have played the customs game put the equipment back in its original state before they go to the shooting game. Explanations are unnecessary, because they have seen the demonstration at the start of the second soccer drill and can start immediately. Although the youngsters carry out 2 now familiar drills simultaneously, you have the time to observe how they are doing. If necessary, he can introduce changes, such as a new rule or an adjustment of the field to the youngsters' level of play.

Activity 3: Small sided drill (3v3)

Organization: At the end of the second drill, everyone collects the equipment and clears up. Everyone then runs to the fields where the small sided drill (3v3) is set up. Explain the drill to the whole group. This is a new drill! After it has been demonstrated, the youngsters play simultaneously on 2 fields.

In the circuit model, a new drill is first explained to the whole group and played by the whole group. During the following session it is played by a smaller group as an element of the circuit model.

Reasons: Here, too, a new drill is again explained to the whole group. You then only have to observe one drill being carried out. This avoids organizational problems. The 3v3 small sided drill is so simple that youngsters can soon carry it out without difficulty. In principle, you can let the youngsters get on with it.

Activity 4: Small sided game (4v4)

Organization: Let the players take down the equipment of the small sided drill. The fields for the small sided game are always set up in advance. The youngsters can set up the goals because the small sided game is the same as in session 1. After the practice vests have been distributed the game can start.

Reasons: The youngsters can again start quickly and they are familiar with the rules. Because this is a familiar soccer format, the coach has more opportunity to observe the players selectively and give advice. He can also take part as a neutral player, who is always on the side of the team in possession.

Activity 5: Cleaning up and closing up together

Session 3

Time (min.)	Drill	Game area	Groups	Players/Grp
-10 - 0	Setting up the equipment			
0 - 5	Tag/kick about		1	12
5 - 35	Shooting game	Scoring and defending	1	4
5 - 35	Customs game	Keeping and winning possession as an individual	1	4
5 - 35	Small sided drill (2v2)	Keeping possession and winning possession as a team	1	4
35 - 55	Small sided game (4v4/2v2)	All game areas	2	8+4
55 - 60	Cleaning up			

Reasons: Session 3 is the first session in which the full circuit model is used.

CHANGEOVERS

The rotation is carried out as follows:

- Take all the players to the field where the first drill is carried out. Let group 1, which starts here, carry out the soccer drill to demonstrate to the others the objective and the rules. Group 1 then continues with the drill.
- Groups 2 and 3 go to the second field. Together with group 3, watch while group 2 carries out the second drill. Group 2 then continues with the drill.
- Finally the third drill is explained only to group 3. Group 3 then continues with the drill.

Changeover (after ten minutes):

- Take group 1 to the second drill. Group 2 is still playing, thus serving as an example for the others. A short explanation of the rules suffices. Group 1 takes the place of group 2.
- Take group 2 to the third drill and repeat the above.

- Take group 3 to the first drill. They have already seen group 1 demonstrate this at the start. Observe to see what they remember and correct them when necessary.
- The second changeover is the same.

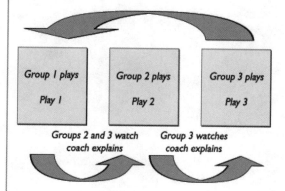

It is a misunderstanding to assume that new soccer drills must be introduced in each coaching session. Youngsters in this age group do not mind repeating familiar drills, provided the drills can be modified and remain challenging. It is the coach's task to use soccer drills that are suitable for the playing level of the youngsters (see chapter 6 - Soccer drills in practice).

Next coaching session

In the next session, it is logical to replace one of the soccer drills that were included for the third time in session 3, for example the shooting game. This can be replaced by a soccer drill from the same theme line, for example the scoring game. This is explained to the whole group, then a smaller group demonstrates it and subsequently continues carrying it out. The other players are divided into 2 groups and carry out the already familiar drills. The coach remains to observe the new drill. After a few minutes he goes to the other groups to change some aspect or give new instructions.

In this way, the circuit model can be introduced without causing the coach any organizational or intrinsic problems. The stock of soccer drills is slowly expanded. And there is always the option of introducing a familiar soccer drill again after a period of time, so that a coaching cycle is created. (see the CD-Rom)

Observant readers will have noted that no comments are made about aspects of soccer during the first coaching sessions. Nor should they be. Only when the circuit model is established is it time to deal with these aspects.

Supervision

As a guide, 3 questions have been formulated to help coaches to obtain a fast overview of how things are going.

1. The first question is: **"Is the game running smoothly?"**
   This question is especially important during the first sessions. Give the players some time to grasp the game objective and the rules of the soccer drill. If, after a while, things are not proceeding as you would wish, take a closer look. Observe closely why things are going wrong and try to solve the problem. Sometimes players deliberately break the rules in order to test how far a coach will let them go or because they cannot win the game otherwise. There are always some players in the group who are bad losers. Perhaps a player has something else on his mind and lack of concentration is the reason that the session is not going smoothly. Tip: Try to contact the parents and reach agreements. This can avert a lot of trouble. It is difficult to pinpoint in advance why a soccer drill does not run smoothly. The coach will have to acquire his own experience. What is important is that the coach clearly explains the rules of conduct and the rules of the game and checks that they are obeyed.

2. The second question that a coach has to ask himself is: **"Are the objectives being achieved?"**
   The rules are clear, but can the players achieve the game objective? For example, do the players succeed in scoring? If they do not, the goal can be made wider or the distance from the goal can be shortened. Organizational changes are

always made in the interests of the game objective. If the players succeed in scoring, they will enjoy themselves more. In shooting and scoring drills, an average of 6 attempts out of 10 should succeed. If only 3 succeed, the distance from the goal is too great. If 8 out of 10 attempts are successful, the shooting distance is too short. The objective must be neither too difficult nor too easy.

3. The third question that a coach has to ask himself is: **"Are the players learning (and having fun)?"**
   If the rules are known and the game objectives are being achieved, the next question is whether the players are learning what they need to learn. In small sided drills, for example, are they getting better at realizing when a teammate is really unmarked? Or, in a shooting drill, are they learning to position themselves better in relation to the ball, so that more shots hit the target? More gifted soccer players must be able to learn more and the situation must be a challenge for them. However, the average and weaker players must also be able to learn, otherwise they will lose their motivation.

In this phase, the coach must give instructions. Their content depends on the objectives of the soccer drill. Such an instruction might be "Look to see where the defender is before you start to run with the ball."

As already mentioned, a play-oriented approach is a prerequisite for participating in a soccer activity. In the U10 phase as a player, but later perhaps as an organizer, coach and/or referee.

Closely associated with this prerequisite is the fun that youngsters experience when they play soccer. Coaching sessions and matches must be organized in such a way that youngsters are able to play and enjoy the game to the maximum. The pleasure of playing, and cooperating, and the effort expended to obtain a good result, are also involved. In short, this is about the fun that players have when they play in line with the objectives of the game. The soccer drill must be aligned to the world of experience of the young players.

Are the players able to score?

Main phases

In a game of soccer, there are 4 main phases:
1. Possession of the ball.
2. Switch when possession is lost.
3. Opposition in possession.
4. Switch when possession is regained.

These main phases form a continuous chain, i.e. the 4th phase (switch when possession is regained) automatically leads to the first phase again (possession).

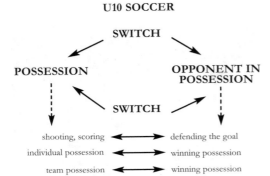

U10 SOCCER

If we look at the game areas, it seems that there are only 2 phases: 'possession' and 'opposition in possession.' The following summary shows that this is not so. One example of this is the instruction: "When you lose the ball, you have to ensure that you get it back as soon as possible." This instruction refers to the switch from the phase 'opposition in possession' to 'possession.'

Coaching aspects

When the moment arrives for the coach to give verbal guidance, his instructions should be short and to the point. The following tips refer to soccer actions in specific situations.

Many coaches cover up their lack of soccer know-how by talking a lot. This is disastrous when coaching young players. A demonstration works faster, is more enjoyable and is also more effective!

For the player in possession:
- Running with the ball when one or more opponents are nearby
  o Try to keep the ball close to your feet, so that no one can take it off you.
  o Try to just tap the ball frequently as you run. You can direct it past defenders more easily then.
- Pushing the ball forward and running with it
  o Try to run forward as fast as possible with the ball.
  o You don't have to touch the ball so often when you want to get forward quickly.
  o Push the ball further in front of you.
- Passing
  o Try to strike the ball with the laces/inside of the foot (briefly demonstrate). You can pass more accurately that way.
  o Try to kick the ball harder/more gently next time.
- Shooting
  o Try to strike the ball with the laces of your boot/the top of your foot. You can shoot harder that way.
  o Try to strike the middle of the ball.
- Receiving the ball
  o Try to stop the ball first
  o Try to get behind the ball if you want to stop it.
  o Try to cushion the ball, otherwise it will bounce off your foot.

For the teammates of the player in possession:
  o Try to stand further apart when your team is in possession.

o Do not get too close to each other.

o Make sure that you are in a position to receive a pass.

For the players who are not in possession:

o Try to block your opponent's path to the goal. Stand between your opponent and the goal.

o Try to win the ball as quickly as possible.

o If we win the ball close to the opposition's goal we might be able to score quickly.

o When you are near your own goal, stand close to your opponent so that he cannot shoot.

o You have to work together to win the ball.

A good example

Finally: the small sided game

After the circuit, each team clears away the equipment from its own field. The 2 fields are then ready for the small sided game. Only the goals may have to be positioned. Usually the coach does this quickly. Then everyone is ready at the same time. After the 2 games have been in progress for a while, the coach tells 2 teams to change fields, so that each team faces a new opponent. The coach has the task of assessing the individual potential of each player. If an instruction is given to an individual, the player must be allowed to experiment. At this age, youngsters should not be given too many instructions. Above all, let the children play. In a small sided game they are confronted with a mass of information all at one time and thus have enough to learn.

Initially the coach can choose small sided drills in which one team has more players than the other, for example of 4v3 with 4 goals. Later, as the players' skills improve, the youngsters can play with equal numbers in each team, for example 4v4 or 7v7.

Equipment

To be able to hold a worthwhile coaching session with this group of players, each group must have a playing area of at least 40 x 40 yards. Two fields can be set up for 2 small sided games. The preceding soccer drills are again set up in the fields. Necessary equipment:

◆ One ball per player
◆ Practice vests, in at least 2 colors
◆ Cones
◆ Marker cones
◆ 3-yard goals or 4v4 goals
◆ Small goals

Equipment. . .

The quantities depend on the number of players.

Number of players

The structure of the circuit model described above is based on twelve players. It can, however, also be used for 10 players. One of the 3 fields is then left open, and the other 2 are used by 2 groups of 5 players. When the groups switch to the next game, one group moves to the open field. Remember that unfamiliar soccer drills should not be played on the open field. The next group must always have an example to watch. When no such example is present, because no one is playing, the coach must explain the soccer drill again. This costs precious time.

Sharing the field

The above circuit model is eminently suitable for a group of ten to fifteen players. The players can be assigned to groups on the basis of the chosen soccer drills (see diagram). At many clubs, however, different teams train at the same time. This may mean that as many as thirty U10 players have to play on one field simultaneously. If this is the case, the above circuit model can be used. The following situation is assumed:

- ◆ Accommodation: Training field (80 x 40 yards)
- ◆ Available time: 60 minutes
- ◆ Number of teams: 4 U10 teams (10 players/team)
- ◆ Total # of players: 40
- ◆ Total # of coaches: 4

Warming up can consist of a game of tag or a kick around.

Time	Sequence	Drill 1 Penalty game	Drill 2 Crossover game	Drill 3 Small sided drill 2v2	Game Small sided game 4v4
5:45 - 6:00	Setup				
6:00 - 6:05	Introduction				
6:05 - 6:18	Round 1	E1	E2	E3	E4
6:18 - 6:31	Round 2	E4	E1	E2	E3
6:31 - 6:44	Round 3	E3	E4	E1	E2
6:44 - 6:57	Round 4	E2	E3	E4	E1
6:57 - 7:00	Take down				

Method

The coaches of the first and second teams (E1 and E2) set up the fields beforehand. The coaches of the third and 4th teams (E3 and E4) clear up afterwards. The sequence of the teams can be changed after a given time, so that the setting up and cleaning up are not always done by the same coaches. In this schedule, each group trains for 60 minutes. No difference is made between the teams! Each coach accompanies his group from drill to drill.

Organization

The penalty game, crossover game and small sided drill are set up in duplicate, otherwise the drills are too crowded.

The fields can be set up as follows:

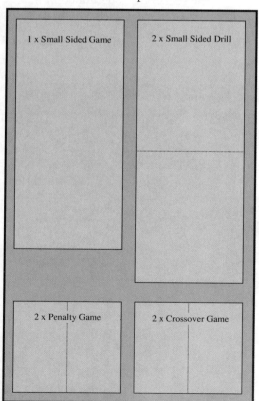

An example:

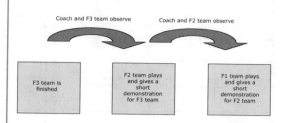

Conditions

More than in the first variant of the circuit model, this method requires the coaches to agree on:

◆ Training times
◆ Setting up and taking down
◆ Planning the content of the session
◆ Sufficient equipment: more cones are needed to play the shooting game with 8 players than with 4.

Advantages

The circuit model has a number of advantages: The coach has a good overview because he only has one group, in which the players are all doing the same thing (compare this with the first session with the first circuit model variant). For the youngsters, it is an honor to be called on to demonstrate a drill for another team. The players in the E2 team can show the E3 team what they have learned. It is up to the coaches to ensure that a good atmosphere is created, in which this can all be carried out without any preconceptions. Negative rivalry must always be avoided!

	Introduction	Shooting and scoring drills	Possession drills (individual)	Small Sided drills	Small sided game
Session 1	Tag/kick around	Shooting game	Customs game		4v4
Session 2	Tag/kick around	Shooting game	Customs game	3v3: line soccer	4v4
Session 3	Tag/kick around	Shooting game	3-lives game	3v3: 4 small goals	4v4
Session 4	Tag/kick around	Scoring game	3-lives game	3v3: 2 medium size goals	4v4
Session 5	Tag/kick around	Scoring game	Chaos game	4v3: line soccer	4v4
Session 6	Tournament	4v4 activities			
Session 7	Tag/kick around	1-2 game	Chaos game	4v3: 4 small goals	4v4
Session 8	etc.				

The above table gives an idea of how a coaching plan might look if the original circuit model - as described above - is selected. Sessions 4 and 5 are in the same line as the preceding sessions. As already mentioned, nothing needs to be changed. It is even advisable not to change anything once the drills are in progress and the players are enjoying themselves. A period can be finished off with, for example, a tournament with 4v4 activities. Of course, coaches can also incorporate drills they have devised themselves.

There is a planner on the CD-ROM "Coaching U10s." You can use this to draw up your own coaching schedule on the basis of the soccer drills described in this book. Coaches can also incorporate drills they have devised themselves.

This chapter contains descriptions of the soccer drills. You can consult chapter 4 to find out how many players are needed in order to carry out a specific soccer drill. The following subjects are treated in their given sequence:

Shooting Drills page 28

Small Sided Drills page 46

Scoring Drills page 33

Small Sided Game page 55

Possession Drills page

SHOOTING DRILLS

Game area: Shooting

Shooting at a target

- ◆ Bull's eye game
  - ◆ 1-2 game

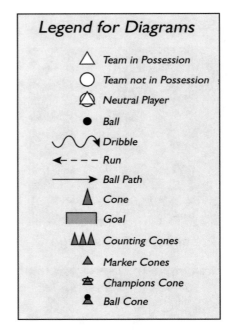

Bull's Eye Game

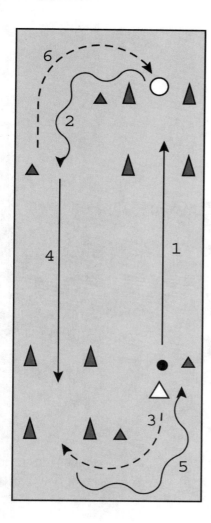

Field
The size of the total playing area is 15 x 5 yards. The scoring zone is 2 x 3 yards.

Description
One player stands between the marker cones and tries to score by kicking the ball into the rectangle (scoring zone). The other player stands behind the scoring zone.

Demonstration
Standing in the starting position, kick the ball as accurately as possible at the scoring zone. The coach can demonstrate this with one player.

Rules
- The ball must be stationary beside the marker cone before the player shoots.
- If the ball stops in the scoring zone, 1 point is scored.
- When the ball is stationary, the player on the other side can take it out of the scoring zone and try to score in the first player's scoring zone.
- The winner is the player who scores 3 points first. The winner then moves his marker cone back.
- The champion (the winner) starts a new series, while the player on the other side continues with his unfinished series.

Adjustments
- After 3 points have been scored, the shooting distance can be increased.
- If 3 attempts are unsuccessful, the shooting distance can be decreased.
- Make the scoring zone larger / smaller / wider / narrower
- When a shooter scores 3 times in the second series, use 3 marker cones to form a triangle inside the scoring zone. The ball must then be kicked into the triangle.
- Form a wall with 3 cones in the line of the shot. The ball must then be kicked over the wall.

Coaching aspects
For the shooter

- Take time to aim
- Take a good look at the scoring zone before you shoot.
- Shoot calmly with the inside of the foot
- Strike the ball properly

Equipment

- 8 cones, 8 marker cones and 1 ball for 2 players.

1-2 game

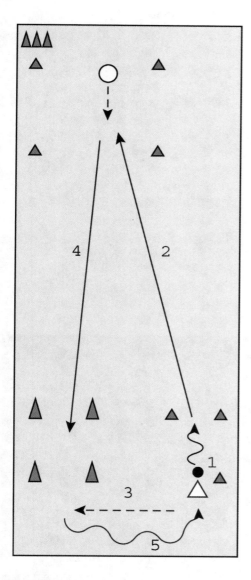

Field

The size of the total playing area is 15 x 6 yards. The 1-2 zone is 4 x 3 yards and the scoring zone 2 x 3 yards.

Description

One player starts beside the marker cone and runs with the ball at his feet toward the gate, then passes to the player in the 1-2 zone, who kicks the ball into the scoring zone on the other side of the field.

Demonstration

Dribble to the gate and pass as accurately as possible to the player in the 1-2 zone, who then kicks the rolling ball into the scoring zone on the other side of the field. The coach should play the role of the player in the 1-2 zone during the demonstration.

Rules

- The dribbler starts at the marker cone and ends at the gate. The dribbler kicks the ball into the 1-2 zone and then runs to a position behind the scoring zone, where he can fetch the ball again.
- The player in the 1-2 zone must kick the rolling ball from the 1-2 zone into the scoring zone.
- The player behind the scoring zone retrieves the ball, runs with it at his feet to the starting point and then starts again.
- If the ball stops in the scoring zone, each player scores 1 point. The player in the 1-2 zone places a counter cone upright.
- When all the cones are upright, the players swap roles.

Adjustments

- The dribbler places the ball beside the gate if he misses the 1-2 zone 3 times.
- If the player in the 1-2 zone misses the scoring zone 3 times, he can control the ball and push it a short distance forward before kicking it into the scoring zone.
- Make the 1-2 zone bigger /smaller/ wider/narrower.
- If the player in the 1-2 zone kicks the ball into the scoring zone 3 times in the second series, use 3 marker cones to

create a triangle in the scoring zone. The ball must then be kicked into the triangle.

Coaching aspects

For the dribbler

- Try to impart enough speed to the ball to be able to kick it into the 1-2 zone.

For the player in the 1-2 zone:

- Position yourself so that it is easy to kick the ball toward the scoring zone.
- Run toward the ball at the right moment so that you can kick it easily toward the scoring zone.

Equipment

- 7 cones (including 3 counter cones), 7 marker cones and 1 ball for 2 players

SCORING DRILLS

Game area: Scoring & defending

Scoring and
preventing others from scoring

- ◆ Shooting game
- ◆ Scoring game

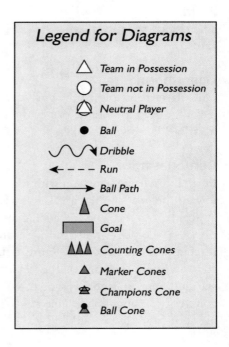

Shooting Game

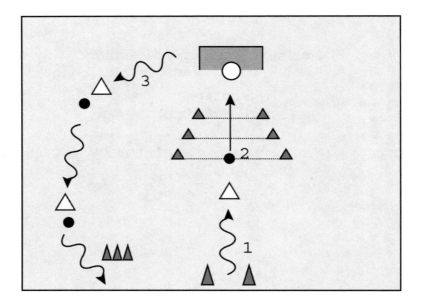

Field

The size of the total playing area is 20 x 15 yards.

Description

One player runs toward the goal with the ball at his feet. Before he passes the imaginary line, he shoots at goal.

Demonstration

From the starting gate, run with the ball toward the goal and the goalkeeper. Shoot at goal before reaching the line. Make it clear that the player must shoot before reaching the marker cones. Retrieve the ball and run round the edge of the field to the starting point. If a goal is scored, stand a counter cone upright and take the following shot from the second line.

Rules

* Waiting players stand in line, each with a ball, beside the starting gate.
* A player must not start his run until the previous player is on his way back to the starting point.
* If a player fails to shoot before crossing the shooting line, he must rejoin the back of the queue of waiting players without shooting.
* If a goal is scored, a cone is stood upright and the player has to take his following shot from the next furthest line.
* If a player fails to score, he must take his following shot from the same line.
* If a player fails to score with 2 successive shots, he must take the following shot from the next closest line.
* After shooting, the shooter retrieves his ball and runs around the edge of the field back to the starting gate. If the goalkeeper saves the ball, he gives it to the shooter. If the shooter shoots wide of the goal, he retrieves the ball himself.
* Change the goalkeeper after 5 non-scoring shots.

Adjustments

- Reduce the distance between the first shooting line and the goal if the players have difficulty kicking the ball over the original distance.
- Place cones in the corners of the goals. If a player knocks over one of these cones, he scores 2 points. If he scores without hitting a cone, he scores 1 point.
- Move the shooting lines to the right or left. The players now have to shoot at goal from an angle.

Coaching aspects

For the shooters:

- Look to see which part of the goal is not covered by the goalkeeper and aim at it. Aim at the empty parts of the goal.
- Position yourself properly relative to the ball. A right-footed player should stand to the left of the ball and a left-footed player to the right.
- Place your support leg alongside or slightly ahead of the rolling ball before shooting.
- Strike the ball firmly.

For the goalkeeper:

- Choose a position from which you can cover as much of the goal as possible with your arms and legs.
- Move toward the approaching ball at the right moment to be able to stop it.

Organization

- 1 medium sized goal.
- Two marker cones are positioned about 6 yards from the goal to mark the first shooting line.
- The following shooting lines are marked about 9 and 10 yards from the goal
- 2 cones mark the starting gate 16 yards

from the goal.
- 3 balls are provided for a group of 4 players.

Equipment

- 1 medium sized goal, 6 marker caps, 5 cones (including 3 counter cones) and 3 balls for 4 players.

Scoring game

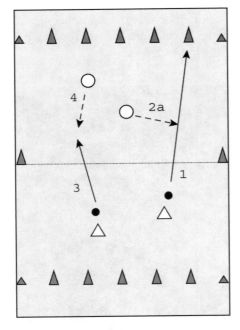

Field

4 marker cones are positioned at the corners of a rectangle measuring 15 x 10 yards.

Description

The players try to knock over the cones on the opposite side of the field, while preventing their own cones from being knocked over. The players must not cross the center line. The game is played with 2 balls.

Demonstration

The coach plays instead of a player and demonstrates how the players must try to defend their own cones and shoot at the cones on the other side. He explains the rules as game situations arise.

Rules

♦ The players must not cross the center line.
♦ The ball can only be played to the opposite side of the field.
♦ When 4 cones have been knocked over, the game is finished.
♦ The winners score 1 point.
♦ If a ball runs over the end line, the player takes a reserve ball and the ballboy retrieves the first ball.

Adjustments

♦ Shorten the distance between the cones and the center line if only 2 shots out of 6 are successful.
♦ Increase the distance if 4 shots out of 6 are successful.
♦ Good players must stay behind an additional line (see follow-up situation).
♦ The next time, the winning team must knock over one cone more.
♦ In place of 2v2, play 3v3 (with one more cone on each side).

Coaching aspects

For the shooter:

♦ Look to see which cones are not defended and aim at one of them.
♦ Wait for a suitable moment to shoot, for example when a defender is distracted by the other ball.
♦ If both players have a ball, one can threaten to shoot, thus drawing the attention of the 2 defenders, and at that moment the other player can shoot.
♦ Wait for a suitable moment to shoot, for example when a defender is distracted by the other ball.
♦ Run forward with the ball before shooting.

For the defender:

- Monitor which cones are still upright and try to cover them.
- Try to prevent the ball from rebounding back into the opposition's half when you stop a shot.

Equipment

- 12 cones, 4 marker cones, 3 vests and 6 balls for 6 players.

Follow-up situation

Scoring game with a third (center) zone. The ball can be dribbled into the center zone to allow the players to get closer to the cones before shooting. Defenders can challenge attackers and win the ball in the center zone.

Organization

- The ball must be played low (below the height of a cone).
- 5 cones are positioned on each end line as targets. The cones are 1 yard apart.
- 2 balls are provided on the field and 4 reserve balls are provided beside the ball-boys.

Equipment

- 14 cones, 4 marker cones, 3 vests and 6 balls for 6 players.

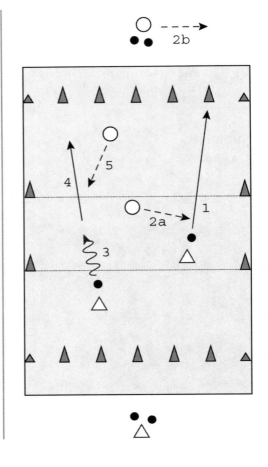

POSSESSION DRILLS

Game area: Keeping possession and winning possession (individual):

Keeping possession
and winning possession
as an individual

- ◆ 3-lives game
- ◆ Chaos game
- ◆ Customs game

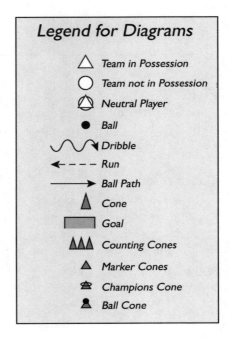

Legend for Diagrams

△ *Team in Possession*

○ *Team not in Possession*

◮ *Neutral Player*

● *Ball*

〰〰➘ *Dribble*

◀ - - - *Run*

──────▶ *Ball Path*

▲ *Cone*

▬▬ *Goal*

▲▲▲ *Counting Cones*

▲ *Marker Cones*

♜ *Champions Cone*

♟ *Ball Cone*

3-lives Game

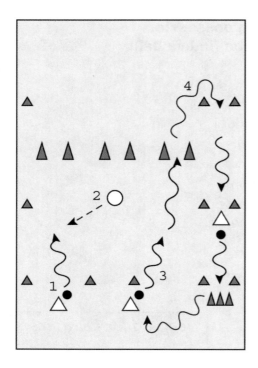

Field

The size of the total playing area is 15 x 10 yards. The ball winning zone measures 10 x 10 yards and the free zone 5 x 10 yards.

Description

Two players, each with a ball, set off at the same time with the aim of dribbling through a goal and then running back with the ball through the corridor and starting again. The defender on the street tries to win the ball by kicking it away from the dribbler's feet.

Demonstration

The coach plays as one of the dribblers, explaining the aims of the game as he does so, and how to score a point and how to restart.

Rules

- The players appoint a ball winner, who positions himself in the ball winning zone.
- The dribblers each take a ball and position themselves at one end of the ball winning zone.
- The dribblers cannot be challenged when they are in the zones at the ends of the street.
- They can always retreat to the zone at the end of the street when they are challenged by the defender.
- When the defender succeeds in tapping the ball away or winning possession from a dribbler, he returns the ball to the dribbler, who goes back to the starting zone, stands a counter cone upright and starts again.
- When 3 counter cones are standing upright, the game is at an end. The defender chooses another ball winner, takes his ball, tips over the cones again and the game starts again.
- A dribbler also loses possession if he leaves the street at one side.
- When a dribbler takes the ball through a goal, he runs back along the corridor to the starting point. When both dribblers have returned, they start again.
- All of the players must take the role of defender at least once.

Adjustments

If the dribblers succeed too easily:

- Make the ball winning zone narrower.
- Start from the champion's gate. The player who dares to start there is a real champion!
- Position another defender in the ball winning zone (the zone must also be made wider).
- Remove one goal (the dribblers decide which one).

If the dribblers have problems:

- Make the ball winning zone wider (max. 15 yards) if 3 out of 5 attempts are intercepted by the defender.
- Introduce a third dribbler.

If the defender wins the ball too easily:

- Make the ball winning zone bigger.
- Increase the size of the goals.

If the defender has problems:

- Make the ball winning zone narrower.
- Allow only one dribbler to cross over at a time.
- Remove a goal (the defender decides which one).

Addition

A defender may focus on winning the ball from the weaker of the 2 dribblers and allow the other dribbler to cross over. In this way he can acquire 3 upright cones faster. In this case, take the counter cones out of the game and play for a given period of time. The weakest player will hang back, using up the ball winner's valuable time. To win the ball as often as possible in the given time, the defender will have to focus on the other dribbler too.

Coaching aspects

For the dribblers:

- Keep the ball close to your feet when you run toward the goals.
- Look to see where the defender/ball winner is standing and choose the best path for crossing over.
- Position yourself between the ball and the defender or return quickly to the starting spot if the ball winner gets too close.

For the ball winner:

- Stay in the middle of the street.
- Block the path of the dribbler and win the ball.
- Move toward the dribblers ('threaten them').

Equipment

- 11 marker cones (including 2 for the champion's gate), 9 cones (including 3 counter cones), 3 balls and 1 practice vest for 4 players.

Chaos game

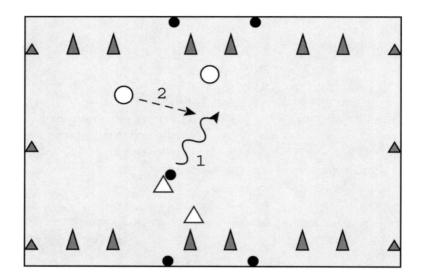

Field

The size of the total playing area is 15 x 10 yards.

Description

There are 2 teams of 2. One of the 2 players defends, while the other tries to score in one of the opposing team's goals.

Demonstration

The coach and another player make up one team. The coach explains the rules as the play proceeds.

Rules

- The two players decide who will defend and who will attack. When a goal is scored, the players of both teams swap roles.
- The game kicks off in the center.
- When a goal is scored, the team that conceded it brings the ball into play from its end line.
- If a player sends the ball out of play, he has to retrieve it himself. The ball is then brought into play again by one of the players of the opposing team.

Adjustments

- Increase the size of the field if there is not enough space to dribble in.
- If too many goals are scored, remove a goal at one end or both ends.

Coaching aspects

For the dribbler (team in possession):

- Keep the ball close to your feet as you run with it.
- Look to see if a goal is not covered, so that you can try to score in it.
- If an opponent challenges, keep your body between the opponent and the ball (screen the ball).
- Dribble away from the opponent into space, to build up speed for a new attack (possibly on another goal).

For the defender (team not in possession):

- Position yourself between your goal and the dribbler. Cover the goal as well as possible.
- Block the path of the dribbler, so you can win the ball.

Addition

If there are an uneven number of players, e.g. 5, 1 player can be a substitute and switch places with the scorer when a goal is scored. One advantage of this is that the composition of the teams constantly changes.

Organization

- 3 goals (each formed by 2 cones) stand in a line at least 4 yards apart. The goals are 1 yard wide.
- 1 ball is provided in the field and there are 4 reserve balls.
- If there are 6 players, each team has a substitute who takes the field in place of the scorer when a goal is scored.

Equipment

- 12 cones, 6 marker cones, 2 practice vests and 5 balls for 4 players.

Customs Game

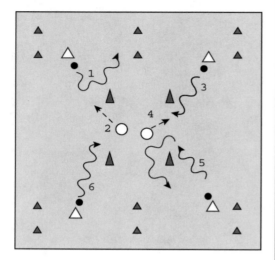

Field

The size of the total playing area is 15 x 15 yards. Four cones are positioned at the corners of a square measuring 5 x 5 yards.

Description

The dribblers (smugglers) try to dribble around their cone in the ball winning zone and return to their start zone, where they cannot be challenged. The ball winners (customs officers) try to win the ball/kick it away from the dribblers' feet.

Demonstration

The coach positions 3 dribblers in the start zone and 2 defenders in the ball winning zone. He plays as a dribbler and demonstrates how the rules apply.

Rules

* After a player has dribbled into the ball winning zone, he can always return to the start zone, where he is safe.
* If a player dribbles around his cone without a defender touching the ball, he scores 1 point.

* The ball winner (customs officer) scores a point if he wins the ball/kicks it away from the dribbler's feet.
* When a dribbler returns to the start zone, he must stop the ball before it crosses the end line, otherwise the point does not count.
* The first player to score 5 points is the winner. The player can be either a dribbler or a ball winner. The game stops. If there is a substitute, he replaces a dribbler.

Adjustments

* Position the cones further apart if the dribblers find it difficult to score points. Reduce the distance between cones if the dribblers score too easily.
* Increase the distance between the start zone and the cone if the dribblers score too easily. Reduce the distance if they find scoring too difficult.
* Each dribbler has his own zone, where he must start and finish. Each player's cone can be further away or closer to his zone.
* If a player wins, his cone is placed one step further away from his start zone the next time.
* The better players are not allowed to retreat to the start zone once they have entered the ball winning zone.
* The better players try to dribble around the most distant cone (this is worth 2 points).

Coaching aspects

For the dribbler:

* Look to see where the ball winner is positioned and choose a suitable moment to dribble to the cone, e.g. when the ball winner is trying to take the ball from another player.

- Keep the ball close to your feet and pay attention to the position and actions of the ball winner.
- If the ball winner challenges, keep your body between the ball winner and the ball (screen the ball).
- Stop the ball when you reach the cone, then turn and dribble the ball back to the starting zone. Stop the ball in the starting zone.

For the ball winner:

- Kick the ball away from the dribbler when the chance arises, especially when he lets the ball run too far away from his feet.
- Watch several dribblers at the same time.

Organization

- 6 marker cones at each end mark a starting zone 2 yards deep (the sidewalk).
- In the ball winning zone are 4 cones at a distance of 6 yards from the starting zone and 6 yards from the sideline.
- 2 vests for the ball winners. 4 balls (1 for each dribbler). If necessary, 1 ball for a substitute.

Equipment

- 12 marker cones, 4 cones, 2 practice vests and 4 balls for 6 players.

Follow-up situation

This game can also be played by 4 players. It is then set up as follows:

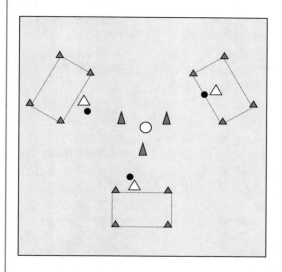

Field

- The total field is 15 x 15 yards
- The free zone is 4 x 3 yards.

Equipment

- 12 marker cones, 3 cones, 3 balls and 1 vest for 4 players.

SMALL SIDED DRILLS

Game area: Keeping possession and winning possession (team):

'Retaining possession
and trying to score

while

the other team tries to win possession
and defend its goal'

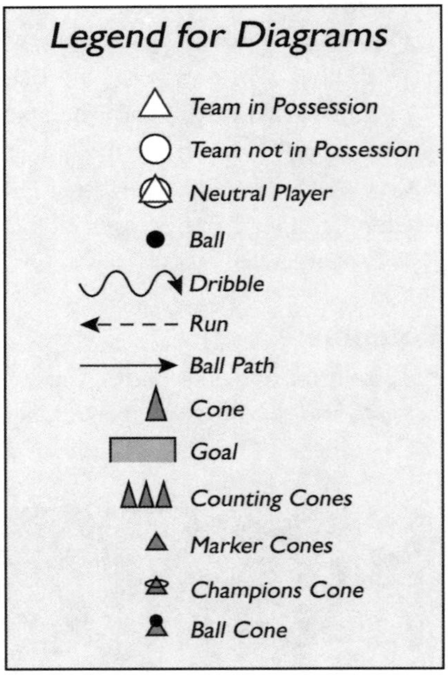

Legend for Diagrams

△ Team in Possession

○ Team not in Possession

◬ Neutral Player

● Ball

〰⟍ Dribble

◀ - - - Run

———▶ Ball Path

▲ Cone

▬ Goal

▲▲▲ Counting Cones

▲ Marker Cones

♟ Champions Cone

♟ Ball Cone

On the way to 4v4

The following small sided drills can be used to progress to 4v4. The choice and sequence depend on the level of skill shown by the U10s. This is a collection of small sided drills, in which the number of players (even or uneven numbers, size of team) and manner of scoring are indicated.

For a number of reasons the small sided game of 4v4 forms the 'end station.'
- A U10 coach does not usually have 14 players in his group during a coaching session and therefore cannot play 7v7.
- For the U10 players, the following small sided drills (and the small sided game of 4v4) provide lots of opportunities for learning to play soccer better.

- 2v1 - line soccer
- 2v1 - 4 small goals
- 2v1 - 2 medium size goals

- 2v2 - line soccer
- 2v2 - 4 small goals
- 2v2 - 2 medium size goals

- 3v2 - line soccer
- 3v2 - 4 small goals
- 3v2 - 2 medium size goals

- 3v3 - line soccer
- 3v3 - 4 small goals
- 3v3 - 2 medium size goals

- 4v3 - line soccer
- 4v3 - 4 small goals
- 4v3 - 2 medium size goals

- 4v4 - line soccer
- 4v4 - 4 small goals
- 4v4 - 2 medium size goals

Criteria
The following criteria apply:

1. From small to larger numbers of players
For novices, there is a big difference between standing on a field together with eight players or fourteen players. Due to the number of players and the size of the field, the players are faced with too many options (have to make too many choices). Too few players are involved in the game and the objectives of the game are not achieved. This gave rise to the idea of playing 4v4 with youngsters of this age.

2. From even to uneven teams
At first the emphasis is on the team in possession. These players must be given the opportunity to experience the first and second secrets, namely playing together as a team and scoring a goal. These are the aspects the coach concentrates on. If the team in possession has one or two players more than the opposing team, its players have a much greater chance of enjoying success. The coach must closely observe the differences in strength and be prepared to make changes in the composition of the team when necessary.

To help the game to flow more smoothly, it is preferable to have one of the better players in the role of the neutral player. Most youngsters feel honored to be chosen as the neutral player. The coach should ensure that all of the players experience this role over the course of time. The weaker players must also have their turn. The coach may decide to switch from even to uneven numbered teams during a small sided drill if the defenders have no chance against the greater number of attackers.

3. From a wide/large to a narrower/smaller scoring zone

It is very difficult to score when the defenders guard the goal very closely. This is true for players of all ages. It is almost impossible to create scoring chances. This is why the scoring zone is initially made very wide and large, and goals can be scored simply by crossing the end line. This is similar to the situation in a game of rugby, in which the players score by carrying the ball across the end line and touching it to the ground. Depending on the level of skill of the players and the ease with which they score, the scoring zone can gradually be made smaller. This is an important aspect for the coach. As it is desirable to change scoring zone if the attackers score too easily or the defenders are always able to prevent the creation of scoring chances.

Coaching aspects in the small sided drills

The youngsters can learn the following:

For the player in possession:
- When you get close to the goal, dribble the ball into the scoring zone or shoot (score).
- Screen the ball and dribble into space, keeping the ball close to your feet (retain possession)
- Play the ball to an unmarked teammate, taking care that it cannot be intercepted by an opponent (combine)
- When you receive the ball in space, control it and keep it close to your feet.

For the teammates of the player in possession:
- Always seek to escape from opponents and take up positions where the player in possession can pass to you
- Run away from the ball to create space if a teammate dribbles toward you
- Take up scoring positions.

For the team that is not in possession (defenders):
- Position yourself between the goal and the opponent and prevent him from scoring by blocking his scoring line
- Block the path of the player in possession and take the ball from him if he allows it to roll too far away from his feet
- Block the passing lines between the player in possession and his teammates.

Demonstration

This is not the place to describe all small sided drills in detail. The following demonstrations show how small sided drills are structured and how they differ from each other.

Small Sided Drill: 3v2 Line Soccer

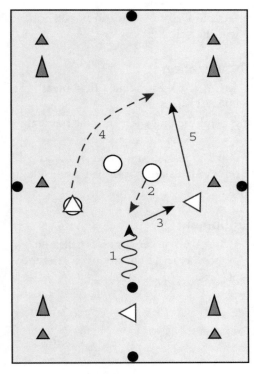

Rules

* Starting on the end line, one player brings the ball into play.
* After a goal is scored, a player of the team that conceded the goal brings the ball into play from his own end line (the opposing players have to stay in their own half until the ball is in play).
* The neutral player is always on the side of the team in possession and can score goals.
* The team that scores 3 goals first wins.
* After about 5 minutes the coach gives a signal and another player becomes the neutral player.
* If a player sends the ball out of play, a player of the other side dribbles the ball into play.

Adjustments

* Vary the size of the field: Increase the size of the field if, for example, possession seems to change every 2 seconds. The players cluster around the ball and there is too little space to combine.

Field

The size of the total playing area is 20 x 12 yards; the scoring zone is 12 x 1 yards.

Description

The team in possession tries to combine to score a goal by dribbling the ball over the end line and stopping it in the scoring zone. The opposing team tries to prevent them from scoring.

Demonstration

The coach demonstrates by taking part as a neutral player together with 4 youngsters. He explains the rules and shows how a goal is scored.

The coach demonstrates as a neutral player

- Vary the number of goals or the size of the scoring zone: Make the zone smaller by, for example, placing 2 small goals on the end line. This gives the defenders more chance of preventing the other team from scoring.
- Vary the number of players: Go from small to larger numbers or from unequal to equal teams whenever the team in possession seems to score too easily and the defenders cannot cope. Switch, for example, from 3v2 to 3v3.

Coaching aspects

For the player in possession

- Dribble the ball over the line in the scoring zone (score).
- Look to see where teammates are in space and play the ball to them out of reach of the defender.
- Run into space with the ball, making simple changes of direction and stops.
- Screen the ball against opponents by positioning yourself between the ball and the opponent, and play the ball to an unmarked teammate.

For the teammates of the player in possession

- Take up positions away from defenders, so that the player in possession can pass to you.
- Run away from a defender, so that the player in possession can pass to you.
- Take up positions other than those of your teammates.

For the team that is not in possession (defenders):

- Position yourself between the goal and the opponent and prevent him from scoring by blocking his scoring line.
- Position yourself so that you (can quickly) cut off passing lines.
- Take up different positions to those of your teammates, so that more passing lines are covered.
- Get close to the player in possession and win the ball if possible.

Organization

- 6 marker cones define a field measuring 20 x 12 yards.
- 2 cones behind each end line mark a scoring zone 1 yards deep.
- A ball is provided in each field and 2 reserve balls are positioned alongside the field.

Equipment

- 4 cones, 6 marker cones, 5 balls and 3 practice vests (2 different colors) for 5 players.

Small Sided Drill: 3v2 with 4 Small Goals

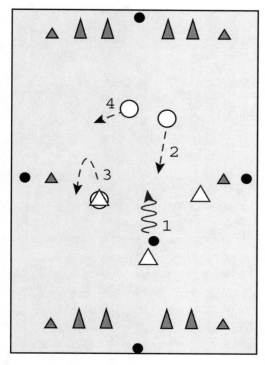

Field
The size of the total playing area is 20 x 15 yards; each goal is 1 yard wide.

Description
The team in possession tries to combine to score a goal by shooting into one of the 2 small goals. The opposing team tries to prevent this and tries to score at the other end of the field.

Demonstration
The coach demonstrates by taking part as a neutral player together with 4 youngsters. He explains the rules and shows how a goal is scored.

Rules
- Starting on the end line, one player brings the ball into play.
- After a goal is scored, a player of the team that conceded the goal brings the ball into play from his own end line (the opposing players have to stay in their own half until the ball is in play).
- The neutral player is always on the side of the team in possession and can score goals.
- The team that scores 3 goals first wins.
- After about 5 minutes the coach gives a signal and another player becomes the neutral player.
- If a player sends the ball out of play, a player of the other side dribbles the ball into play.

Look first, then pass

Adjustments

- Vary the size of the field: Increase the size of the field if, for example, possession seems to change every 2 seconds. The players cluster around the ball and there is too little space to combine.
- Vary the number of goals or the size of the scoring zone: Place a junior goal on the end line or enlarge the scoring zone by playing line soccer.
- Vary the number of players: Go from small to larger numbers or from odd to even numbered teams whenever the team in possession seems to score too easily and the defenders cannot cope. Switch, for example, from 3v2 to 3v3.

Coaching aspects

For the player in possession

- Shoot when you are near the goal (score).
- Look to see where teammates are in space and play the ball to them out of reach of the defender.
- Run into space with the ball, making simple changes of direction and stops.
- Screen the ball against opponents by positioning yourself between the ball and the opponent, and play the ball to an unmarked teammate.

For the teammates of the player in possession

- Take up positions away from defenders, so that the player in possession can pass to you.
- Run away from a defender, so that the player in possession can pass to you.
- Take up positions other than those of your teammates.

For the players who are not in possession/defenders:

- Position yourself between the goal and the opponent and prevent him from scoring by blocking his scoring line.
- Position yourself so that you (can quickly) cut off passing lines.
- Take up different positions to those of your teammates so that more passing lines are covered.
- Get close to the player in possession and win the ball if possible.

Organization

- 6 marker cones define a field measuring 20 x 15 yards.
- 8 cones define the small goals; each goal is one yard wide.
- A ball is provided in each field and 4 reserve balls are positioned alongside the field.

Equipment

- 8 cones, 6 marker cones, 5 balls and 3 practice vests (2 different colors) for 5 players.

Small Sided Game: 3v2 with 2 Medium Size Goals

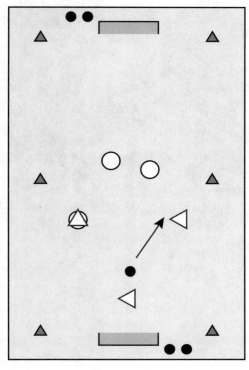

△ ↑　○ ↓　⬙ = **chameleon**

Field

The size of the total playing area is 20 x 15 yards.

Description

The team in possession tries to combine to score a goal by shooting into the junior goal. The opposing team tries to prevent this and tries to score at the other end of the field.

Demonstration

The coach demonstrates by taking part as a neutral player together with 4 youngsters. He explains the rules and shows how a goal is scored.

Rules

* Starting on the end line, one player brings the ball into play.
* After a goal is scored, a player of the team that conceded the goal brings the ball into play from his own end line (the opposing players have to stay in their own half until the ball is in play).
* The neutral player is always on the side of the team in possession and can score goals.
* The team that scores 3 goals first wins.
* After about 5 minutes the coach gives a signal and another player becomes the neutral player.
* If a player sends the ball out of play, a player of the other side dribbles the ball into play.

Adjustments

* Vary the size of the field: Increase the size of the field if, for example, possession seems to change every 2 seconds. The players cluster around the ball and there is too little space to combine.
* Vary the number of goals or the size of the scoring zone: Place 2 small goals on the end line or enlarge the scoring zone by playing line soccer.
* Vary the number of players: Go from small to larger numbers or from unequal to equal teams whenever the team in possession seems to score too easily and the defenders cannot cope. Switch, for example, from 3v2 to 3v3.

Coaching aspects

For the player in possession

* Shoot when you are near the goal (score).
* Look to see where teammates are open and play the ball to them out of the reach of the defender.

- Run into open space with the ball, making simple changes of direction and stops.
- Screen the ball against opponents by positioning yourself between the ball and the opponent, and play the ball to an unmarked teammate.

For the teammates of the player in possession

- Take up positions away from defenders, so that the player in possession can pass to you.
- Run away from a defender, so that the player in possession can pass to you.
- Take up positions other than those of your teammates.

For the team that is not in possession (defenders):

- Position yourself between the goal and the opponent and prevent him from scoring by blocking his scoring line.
- Position yourself so that you (can quickly) cut off passing lines.
- Take up different positions to those of your teammates so that more passing lines are covered.
- Get close to the player in possession and win the ball if possible.

Organization

- 6 marker cones define a field measuring 20 x 15 yards.
- A ball is provided in each field and 2 reserve balls are positioned alongside the field.

Equipment

- 2 medium size goals, 6 marker cones, 5 balls and 3 practice vests (2 different colors) for 5 players.

SMALL SIDED GAME

All game areas

'Retaining possession individually or as a team
and trying to score

while the opposing team

tries to disrupt the play or gain possession
and defend its goal'

The previous section was devoted to small sided drills with a number of variations. These small sided drills are elements of a theme line. The small sided game of 4v4 is generally regarded as the end point of U10 coaching with the circuit model. It is often played on Saturday mornings in consultation with other local clubs. The small sided game of 4v4 is described in more detail in the following section.

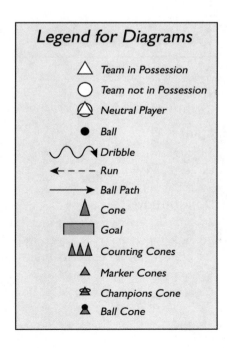

Legend for Diagrams

△   Team in Possession

◯   Team not in Possession

⬯   Neutral Player

●   Ball

〰〰   Dribble

← – – –   Run

———➤   Ball Path

▲   Cone

▭   Goal

▲▲▲   Counting Cones

▲   Marker Cones

♔   Champions Cone

♟   Ball Cone

Small Sided Game: 4v4

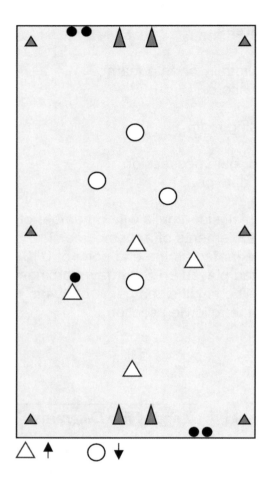

Demonstration

Let 8 players play the game. Explain the main rules on the basis of the situations that arise as they play.

Rules

* The game begins in the center of the field with a kick off. After each goal the ball is brought back into play from the end line beside the goal.
* If the ball rolls out of play, it is kicked into play from the point where it went out. Goals cannot be scored directly from a kick into play.
* The ball can be kicked or dribbled into play from the end line.
* Corners are taken from the corner point.

Coaching aspects

For the player in possession

* Shoot when you are near the goal (score).
* Screen the ball and run into space, keeping the ball close to your feet (keeping possession).
* Pass to a teammate, keeping the ball out of reach of a defender (combining).
* When you receive the ball in space, control it and keep it close to your feet.

Field

Six cones mark a field measuring 40 x 20 yards; the goal is 3 x 1 yards.

Description

2 teams of 4 players play against each other. Both teams try to score and prevent the opposing team from scoring. The teams play without a goalkeeper.

For the teammates of the player in possession:

- Always seek to escape from opponents and take up positions where the player in possession can pass to you
- Run away from the ball to create space if a teammate dribbles toward you
- Take up scoring positions.

For the defenders:

- Position yourself between the goal and the opponent and prevent him from scoring by blocking his scoring line
- Block the path of the player in possession and take the ball from him if he allows it to roll too far away from his feet
- Block a passing line.

Organization

- Place a 4v4 goal, or use 2 cones to create a goal 3 yards wide, on each end line.
- 4 practice vests and a ball are provided in the field and 2 reserve balls are provided beside each goal.
- If there are 10 players in the group, play with 2 teams of 5 players or with 2 teams of 4 and a substitute for each team.

Equipment

- 6 marker cones, 4 cones (or 2 4v4 goals), 8 practice vests (2 different colors) and 5 balls for 8 players.

This chapter is about how U10s can play 4v4 and what rules can be applied. First of all, however, a few words to prevent any misunderstandings.

- For the players, 4v4 is an end in itself. They want to win the small sided game and play as well as possible.
- The person in charge (coach, supervisor, physical education teacher, parent, com mittee member) can view 4v4 as a means of helping youngsters to play soccer better.

Content and organization of 4v4 activities

- U10s play a series of 6 4v4-teams at home and away. This means that they play on 10 different days.
- On the day of each match, each club's U10 players are split into 2 teams of 4.
- There are therefore 4 teams of 4 in all.
- Each team plays each of the other teams once.
- Field : length 40 yards
  (or 35 or even 30 yards, depending on the level of the players)
  : width 20 yards
- Goals: width 3 yards
  : height 1 yard

(The goals must not be smaller, otherwise they can be defended too easily by 1 player.)

- Playing time : 2 x 7.5 minutes
- Ball size : 3
  (Maximum weight 320 grams)
- Each activity is completed by a penalty series, with each player taking a penalty from a distance of 7 yards from the goal.
- At the end of the series of games, all participating teams take part in a final 4v4 tournament. One team wins the tournament and all the players are pre-

sented with a memento of the series of 4v4 activities.

Marking the fields

- It is useful to set up 2 fields, starting in the corners of the big field. This means that the existing side and end lines can be used.

The following aids can be used to mark the lines:

- marker cones
- cones
- tape
- white lines
- Small portable goals (3 yards wide and 1 yard high), or cones, with or without a crossbar, can be used.
- If the club has 4 '5 x 2 goals,' 4v4 with 2 goalkeepers can be played (i.e. 5v5).
- It is advisable to set up 2 exactly equal fields.

'Penalty goal'

It is advisable to assign the 'penalty goal' a place on the field where it can be used immediately when the small sided game of 4v4 is finished. This must be a place where there is no risk to the youngsters as they play 4v4. The edge of the penalty area is perhaps best.

Rules of 4v4

The idea of the game is that the play should be as continuous as possible, and when there is a stoppage the game should be restarted as quickly as possible. The following rules apply:

- Goals can be scored from anywhere on the field.
- There are no goalkeepers.
- One team starts the game by kicking or dribbling the ball into play from the end line.
- When a goal is scored, the game is restarted by kicking or dribbling the ball into play from the end line.
- After a foul, play is restarted with a free kick.
- If the ball rolls over the side line, the game is restarted by kicking the ball into play. This is faster and easier than restarting with a throw in.
- If an attacker sends the ball over the end line, the game is resumed by kicking or dribbling the ball into play from the end line.
- If a defender sends the ball over the end line, the game is resumed with a corner kick. Teach the players to take short corners with the defenders standing at least 5 yards from the ball, so that positional play resumes as quickly as possible. No high crosses should be allowed at such a short distance in front of such a small goal.
- A goal cannot be scored directly from a kick into play from the end or side lines.
- At each restart, the opposing team's players must stand at least 5 yards from the ball.
- If a player handles the ball to prevent a goal, a penalty is awarded. This must be taken from a spot 15 yards from the goal, without a goalkeeper.
- A goal can be scored as follows:
- If cones without a crossbar are used:
  i.   The ball must roll between the cones.
  ii. The ball may touch the cones.
  iii. If a cone falls over, the goal does not count!
- If cones with a crossbar are used:
  iv. If the ball passes through the goal and none of the cones fall over.
- Other goals:
  v.   No explanation needed.

Match program

- It is advisable to draw up the match program beforehand, so that everyone knows when they are playing as soon as they arrive.
- The team leaders should copy the plan or receive a copy from the organizers. The activities will proceed more smoothly and the available time will be used as efficiently as possible.

Number of players

- Irrespective of the numbers of players, 4v4 must always be played, except when 4v4 with goalkeepers is played.
- If a team has 5 players, they must all take turns at being the substitute.
- If a team only has 3 players, 3v3 is played or a player is borrowed from another team.

Practice Vests

- If 2 teams from the same club play against each other, practice vests must be used. The home team must therefore ensure that 10 to 12 vests are available.

Start and finish signal

- It is advisable for the start and end to be signaled centrally.

Referee

- There is no need to have one referee for each field.
- A coach or a parent can act as a supervisor. The idea is that the youngsters should spend as much time playing as possible. They learn what is and is not allowed and can make refereeing decisions themselves. In cases of doubt and/or differences of opinion on the field, the referee's decision is binding.

Breaks

- This is up to the organizers. It must be borne in mind that the next team may need to use the field.

Penalties

- All players can take a penalty, in line with how this is organized after their game finishes.

Layout

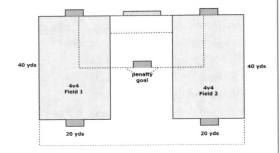

MATCH PROGRAM FOR THE 4V4 TOURNAMENT

Participating teams:

A: _____

B: _____

C: _____

D: _____

Time	Match		Field
00.00- 00.15	A - B - _____		1
00.00- 00.15	C - D - _____		2
00.15- 00.30	A - D - _____		1
00.15- 00.30	B - C - _____		2
00.40- 00.55	C - A - _____		1
00.40- 00.55	D - B - _____		2

8 WHY 7V7?

At one time, a game of soccer was always a game between 2 teams of 11 players, irrespective of how old the players were. As soon as youngsters joined a club, they were 'thrown in at the deep end.' For a number of reasons, this is most inadvisable.

1) Youngsters are usually between 5 and 8 years old when they start to play soccer. At this age, the main priority is for them to 'master' the ball. 'The ball must be your best friend.' In a game of 11v11, it is clear that the number of ball contacts of many of the players is minimal. Given that repetition - in this case, lots of ball contacts - is one of the most important learning concepts, this is obviously not a satisfactory state of affairs. Analysis of such games showed that several youngsters did not touch the ball even once!

2) Not only are too many players involved in games of 11v11, so that the youngsters are faced with too many options, but the field is also far too big. The youngsters drown in a sea of space. It is difficulty for them to bridge the distances involved. Soccer is about scoring goals and preventing goals from being scored. If players are scarcely able to reach the opposing team's goal, then they unable to play soccer properly. There is no relationship between offense and defense. The players cannot transfer the ball fast enough from one end of the field to the other. They cannot learn under these circumstances!

In short, the number of players (11v11) and the size of the field (full soccer field) ensure that the number of ball contacts is minimal, the number of options is too large, the number of players involved in the play is too small and the game objectives are not realized. In practice, this

means that U10s play 7v7 in their weekly competitive games.

Small numbers = better overview